# What If You Get Lost?

### Elizabeth Kernan

The Rosen Publishing Group, Inc.
New York

What if you get lost?

Ask a police officer for help.

Go to a telephone if there are no police officers.

Call 911 to get help.

Stay in one place.

A police officer will find you and take you home.

# Words to Know

911

police officer

telephone